My Adventure with Fluffy

David Campos as told to Robert Kaufman

Contents

Rigby
A Harcourt Achieve Imprint

www.Rigby.com
1-800-531-5015

The Adventure Begins

I'm David and this is Fluffy. Last week we went on a trip to Los Angeles, California.

Come along with us and
we'll show you
our favorite places!

The Ocean

The first place we visited
was the ocean.
An ocean is a large body
of salt water.

At the ocean, Fluffy and I
had fun in the sun.
We breathed in the fresh air
and splashed in the waves.

We liked playing on the beach. Fluffy and I had a great time building sandcastles.

Did You Know?

The Pacific Ocean is
the largest ocean
in the world.
It covers about
one third of Earth!

PACIFIC
OCEAN

Mountains

Next we went
to the mountains.
A mountain is
a very high piece of land.

Fluffy and I hiked
to the top of a mountain.
The air up there
was crisp and cool.
What a sight!

We also visited Mount Baldy.
During the winter,
it is covered with snow.
Fluffy and I love to play
in snow!

Did You Know?

Mount Baldy got its name because wind and avalanches have destroyed all the trees and plants at the top, making it look like a bald head.

Forests

Fluffy and I also went to Angeles National Forest. A forest is an area of land covered with many trees.

Fluffy and I ran along
the paths in the forest.
Once we entered the forest,
I felt like I was far
from the city.

Next we went
to Sequoia National Park.
The sequoia trees there are
the largest trees in the world.

Did You Know?

The General Sherman sequoia tree is about as tall as 21 elephants.

The Desert

After we left the forest,
I took Fluffy to the desert.
A desert is a hot, dry area
that does not get much rain.

Fluffy and I looked for cacti and animals while we were in the desert.

Our favorite desert is
Joshua Tree National Park.
Spring is the best time
to go there
because the air is cool.

Did You Know?

Joshua trees only
grow in four states:
California, Arizona,
Utah, Nevada.

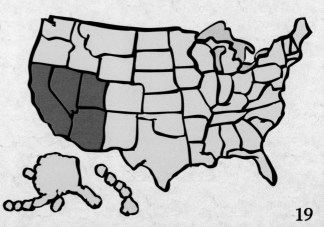

Back Home

Fluffy and I love adventures, and we had a great time. But sometimes we just like to relax at home.

Common Landforms

Forest

Ocean

Mountains

Desert

Glossary

desert a hot, dry area that does not get much rain

forest an area of land covered with many trees

mountain a very high piece of land

ocean a large body of salt water